ZOOM

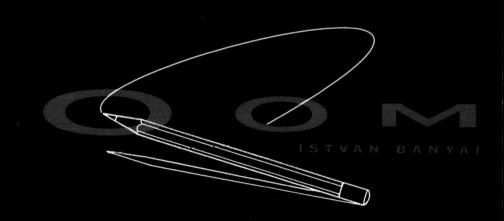

ISTVAN BANYAI

VIKING

TO MY WIFE, KATALIN, AND OUR SON, SIMON CHRISTOPHER

VIKING
PUBLISHED BY THE PENGUIN GROUP
PENGUIN BOOKS USA INC., 345 HUDSON STREET, NEW YORK, NEW YORK 10014, U.S.A.
PENGUIN BOOKS LTD, 27 WRIGHTS LANE, LONDON W8 5TZ, ENGLAND
PENGUIN BOOKS AUSTRALIA LTD, RINGWOOD, VICTORIA, AUSTRALIA
PENGUIN BOOKS CANADA LTD, 10 ALCORN AVENUE, TORONTO, ONTARIO, CANADA M4V 3B2
PENGUIN BOOKS (N.Z.) LTD, 182-190 WAIRAU ROAD, AUCKLAND 10, NEW ZEALAND

PENGUIN BOOKS LTD, REGISTERED OFFICES: HARMONDSWORTH, MIDDLESEX, ENGLAND

FIRST PUBLISHED IN 1995 BY VIKING, A DIVISION OF PENGUIN BOOKS USA INC.

19 20 18

COPYRIGHT © ISTVAN BANYAI, 1995
ALL RIGHTS RESERVED

LIBRARY OF CONGRESS CATALOGING-IN-PUBLICATION DATA
BANYAI, ISTVAN.
ZOOM / BY ISTVAN BANYAI.   P. CM.
SUMMARY: A WORDLESS PICTURE BOOK PRESENTS A SERIES OF SCENES, EACH ONE FROM
FARTHER AWAY, SHOWING, FOR EXAMPLE, A GIRL PLAYING WITH TOYS WHICH IS ACTUALLY
A PICTURE ON A MAGAZINE COVER, WHICH IS PART OF A SIGN ON A BUS, AND SO ON.
ISBN 0-670-85804-8
[1. VISUAL PERCEPTION—FICTION.]   I. TITLE.
PZ7.B22947Zo 1995 [E]—DC20 94-33181 CIP AC

MANUFACTURED IN CHINA